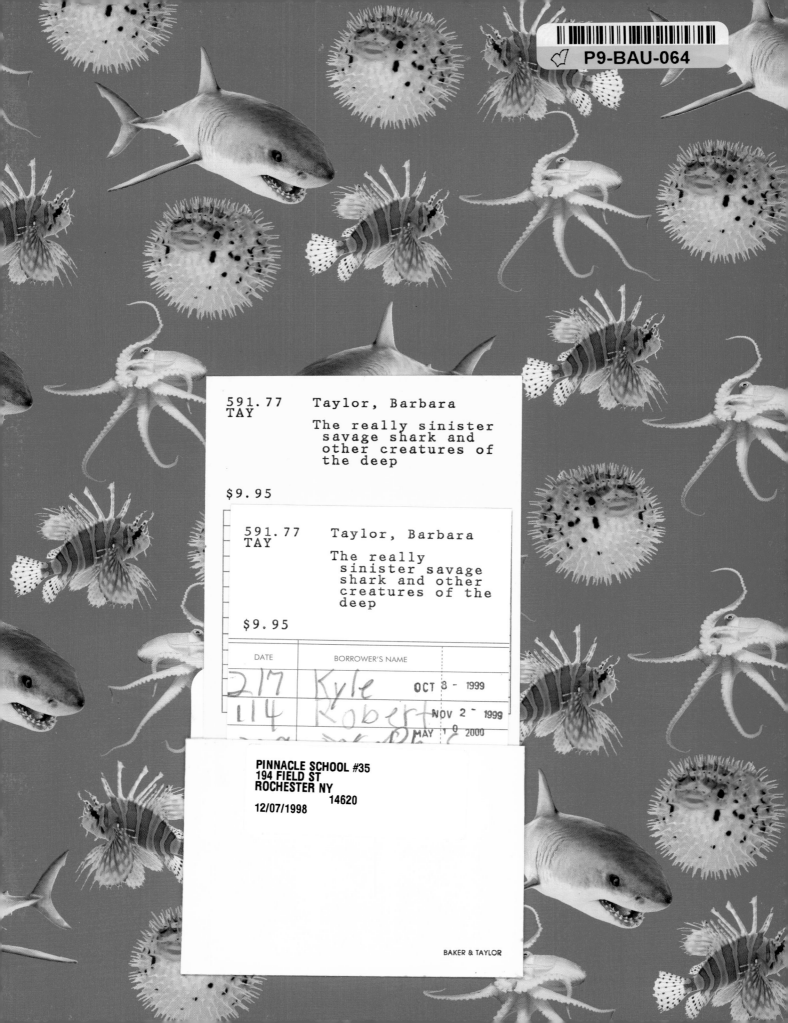

A DK PUBLISHING BOOK

Senior Editor Susan Peach
Art Editor Marcus James
Editor Katherine Moss
Designer Dean Price
US Editor Camela Decaire
DTP Designer Almudena Díaz

Managing Editor Jane Yorke
Managing Art Editor Chris Scollen
Production Kate Oliver
Picture Research James Clarke,
Sally Hamilton
Jacket Design Mike Buckley

First American Edition, 1997
2 4 6 8 10 9 7 5 3 1

Published in the United States by
DK Publishing, Inc., 95 Madison Avenue
New York, New York 10016

Visit us on the World Wide Web at
http://www.dk.com
Copyright © 1997 Dorling Kindersley
Limited, London

Published in Great Britain by
Dorling Kindersley Limited.

A catalog record for this book is available
from the Library of Congress.

ISBN: 0-7894-2050-3
Color reproduction by Flying Colours.
Printed in Italy by L.E.G.O.

The publisher would like to thank the following for
their kind permission to reproduce their photographs:
t = top, b = bottom, l = left, r = right, c = center.

The Goldfish Bowl, Oxford (Deadly Poisons: tr);
Robert Harding Picture Library (Deadly Poisons: br);
Image Bank/ Al Giddings Images Inc. (Great White
Monster: bl); Natural History Museum (Teeth and
Tusks: tr); NHPA/ Henry Ausloos (Teeth and Tusks:
bl); Oxford Scientific Films/ Norbert Wu (Scary
Sharks: tl); Planet Earth Pictures (Armed and
Dangerous: br)/ Ken Lucas (Scary Sharks: ca,
Deadly Poisons: bc); Tony Stone Images/ Ben
Osbourne (Teeth and Tusks: cb)/ Mike Steverns
(Teeth and Tusks: tr); Zefa (jacket: br).

Great White Monster

Armed and
Dangerous

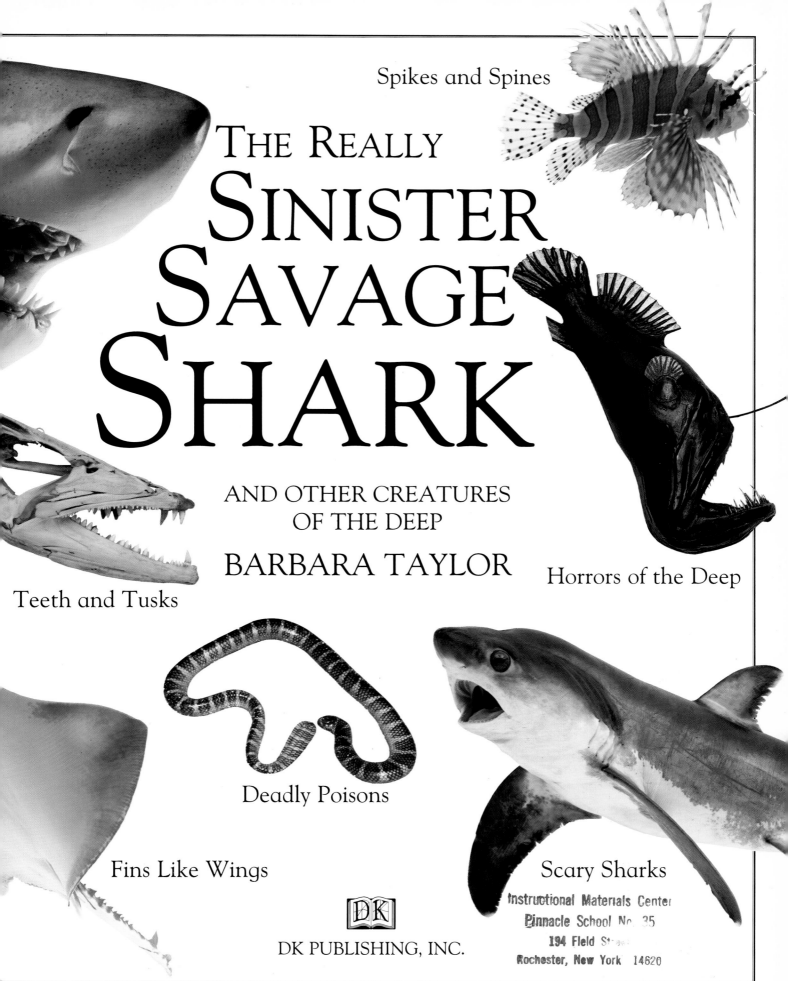

Spikes and Spines

THE REALLY
SINISTER
SAVAGE
SHARK

AND OTHER CREATURES
OF THE DEEP

BARBARA TAYLOR

Teeth and Tusks

Horrors of the Deep

Deadly Poisons

Fins Like Wings

Scary Sharks

DK

DK PUBLISHING, INC.

GREAT WHITE MONSTER

This huge and powerful hunter can eat seals whole and bite a person in half! The shark's razor-sharp teeth can viciously slice through its victims.

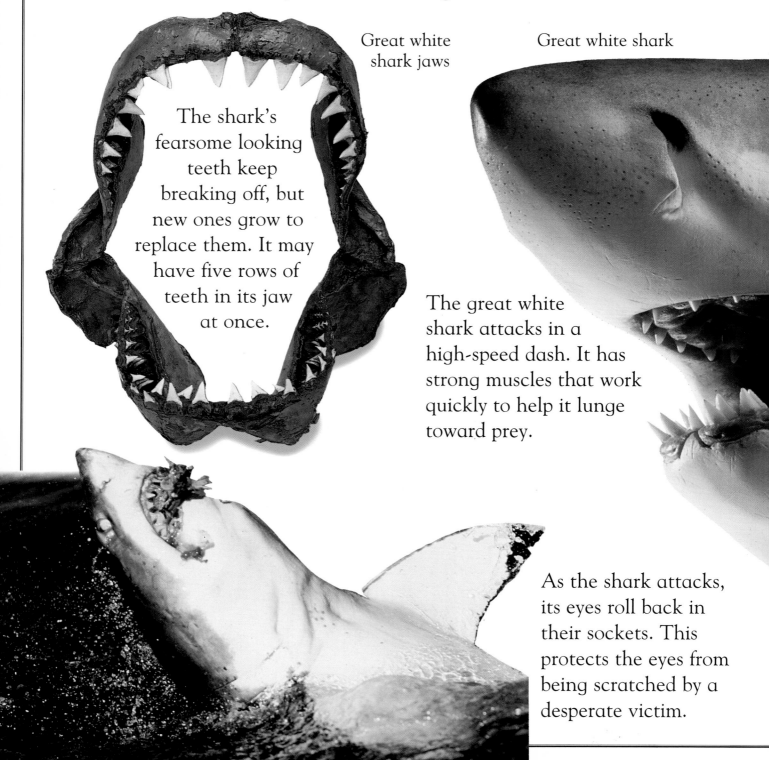

Great white shark jaws

Great white shark

The shark's fearsome looking teeth keep breaking off, but new ones grow to replace them. It may have five rows of teeth in its jaw at once.

The great white shark attacks in a high-speed dash. It has strong muscles that work quickly to help it lunge toward prey.

As the shark attacks, its eyes roll back in their sockets. This protects the eyes from being scratched by a desperate victim.

The color of the great white shark makes it hard to see in the water. It can sneak up on its victims and take them by surprise.

Pores on the great white's snout detect electrical signals from prey.

SCARY SHARKS

Hammerhead shark

Sharks are streamlined hunters that slice quickly through water. They can smell blood from injured prey up to 1,640 ft (500 m) away!

Cookie-cutter shark

Many sharks, such as this leopard shark, are harmless to humans. More people die from bee stings or lightning strikes than from shark attacks.

The cookie-cutter has fat lips that stick tight to prey. It drives its sharp teeth into a victim, then twists in a circle to remove a cookie-shaped meal of flesh.

Leopard shark

Sharks can detect one part of blood in a million parts of water.

The thresher shark has by far the longest tail of any known shark. It uses its tail like a whip to stun or kill small fish and other prey.

The hammerhead shark's favorite foods are stingrays and catfish, which have poisonous spines! It does not seem to mind being stung and must be immune to the poison.

The hammer-shaped head swings from side to side as the shark swims.

The part of a shark's brain that controls smell is twice as large as the rest.

Thresher shark

Horn sharks

Horn sharks have huge, piglike nostrils. Like pigs, they are very good at picking up the scent of food.

ARMED AND DANGEROUS

Tentacles may look like extra arms, but beware! These creatures are all equipped with suckers and stings on their tentacles for capturing unsuspecting victims.

An octopus seizes prey with its tentacles, then releases poison to paralyze the victim. Eight arms covered with about 200 suckers let it grab fish and even other octopuses!

If an octopus loses a tentacle, a new one will grow to take its place.

Sea cucumber

The long arms curl around a victim and prevent any escape.

The sticky tentacles of this sea cucumber trap tiny plants and animals on a coral reef. The sea cucumber sucks food off the feathery tentacles with its fleshy lips.

A sea anemone's colorful tentacles conceal deadly stinging spines that inject poison into its prey.

Dahlia anemone

Squid have horny beaks for tearing apart prey.

Squid

A squid uses its eight arms to hold prey in place while it delivers a poisonous bite.

Common octopus

There are two rows of powerful suckers under each arm.

This jellyfish can kill a person in just a few minutes using the millions of poisonous stings on its tentacles.

Box jellyfish

FINS LIKE WINGS

Beware of flat-as-a-pancake shark relatives called rays, hiding on the seabed! Some have a sting in the tail, while others can give painful electric shocks.

There are over 160 different kinds of stingrays. Most have at least one poisonous spine on their tail for stinging enemies.

The thornback ray has vicious spines on its back and tail for defense. It is patterned on top to keep it camouflaged from predators and prey.

Thornback ray

Rays are often plain underneath since this side is buried in the seabed.

Rays have huge, winglike fins joined to their heads. They flap their wings up and down to swim along.

Undulate ray

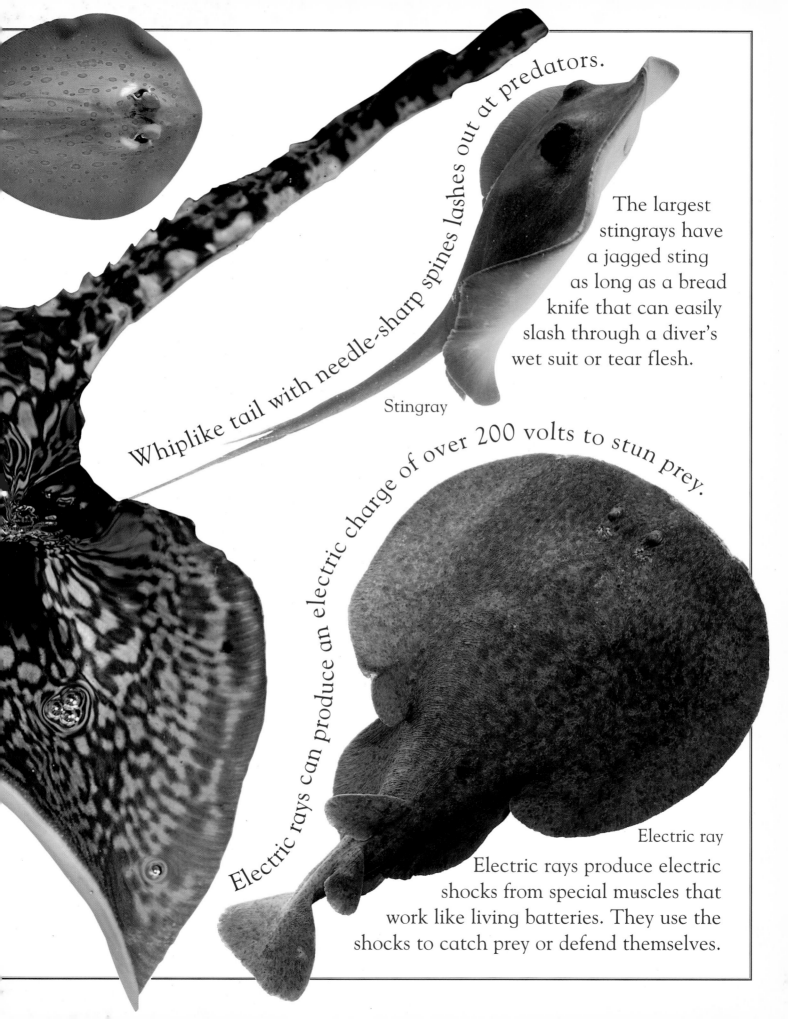

Whiplike tail with needle-sharp spines lashes out at predators.

The largest stingrays have a jagged sting as long as a bread knife that can easily slash through a diver's wet suit or tear flesh.

Stingray

Electric rays can produce an electric charge of over 200 volts to stun prey.

Electric ray

Electric rays produce electric shocks from special muscles that work like living batteries. They use the shocks to catch prey or defend themselves.

TEETH AND TUSKS

With their powerful, pointed teeth and tusks or razor-sharp saws and swords, these sea animals can slash and stab at enemies and rip apart prey.

School of barracuda

Sawfish and swordfish use their amazing noses for defense and killing prey. The swordfish's sharp nose can pierce the hull of a boat.

Barracuda skull

Sawfish nose bone

Swordfish nose bone

Walruses cause serious wounds when fighting with their tusks.

The length of a walrus's tusks shows how important it is in a group. The male walrus with the biggest tusks is usually the boss.

A ribbon eel seizes its prey with a snap of its needle-sharp teeth.

Ribbon eel

Walrus

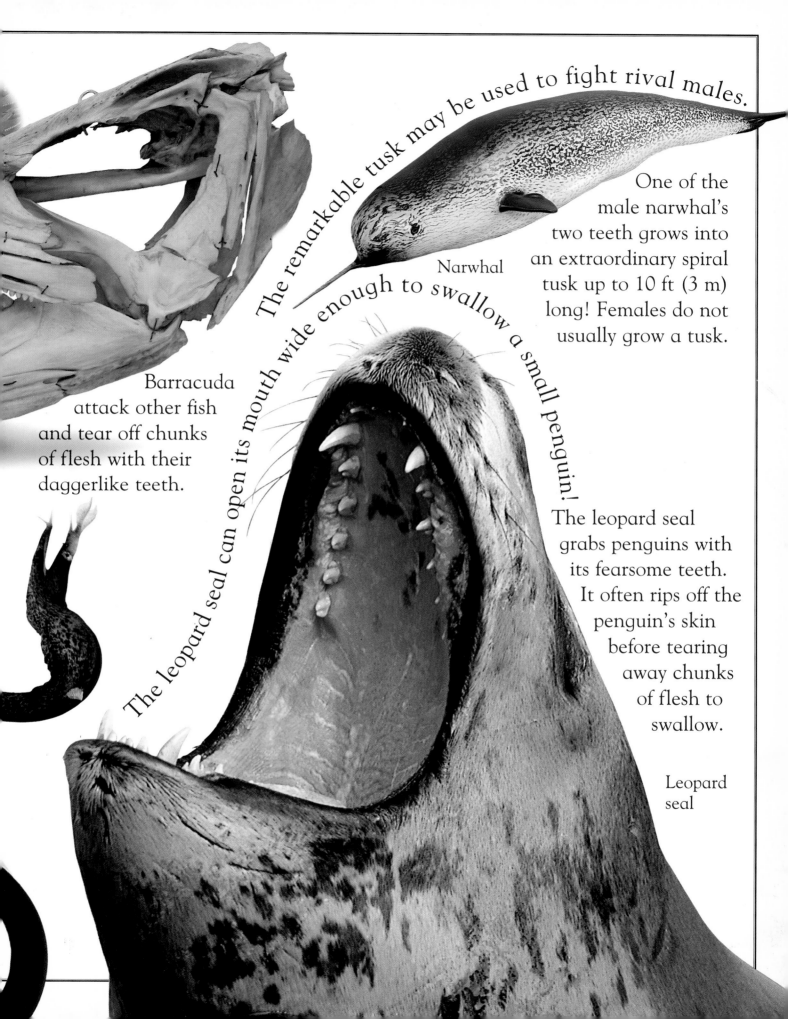

The remarkable tusk may be used to fight rival males.

One of the male narwhal's two teeth grows into an extraordinary spiral tusk up to 10 ft (3 m) long! Females do not usually grow a tusk.

Narwhal

Barracuda attack other fish and tear off chunks of flesh with their daggerlike teeth.

The leopard seal can open its mouth wide enough to swallow a small penguin!

The leopard seal grabs penguins with its fearsome teeth. It often rips off the penguin's skin before tearing away chunks of flesh to swallow.

Leopard seal

SPIKES AND SPINES

These fish are all armed to the teeth! Beneath their fins lurk cruel spines, deadly poisons, and vicious stings.

The needle-sharp spines of a stripy lionfish are full of deadly poison. When enemies see the bright patterns on this fish, they know it signals danger.

Lionfish are fierce predators of smaller fish.

Lionfish

Weever fish

Keep well away from weever fish! If you step on one sitting on the seabed, it can give you a very painful sting!

Grooves in spines contain deadly poison.

Scorpion fish

This fish has a row of poisonous spines along its back. Anything that presses on the sharp spines gets an injection of deadly poison.

Porcupine fish

A frightened porcupine fish puffs up its body to make its sharp spines stick out. Enemies usually decide to leave this spiky ball alone!

Inflated porcupine fish

This prickly mouthful is impossible for enemies to swallow.

Long, lacy fins hide the poison spines.

HORRORS OF THE DEEP

Some deep-sea fish use glowing "fishing rods" to lure prey within easy snatching distance in the depths of the cold, dark ocean.

Hatchet fish

The weird eyes of the gigantura may help pick up the glowing light given off by the fish it preys on in the pitch-black water.

Gigantura

Glowing patches inside the mouth of a hatchet fish draw prey right into its deadly jaws.

Imagine having a fishing line on the end of your nose! The whipnose uses its fishing line to lure prey up close to its mouth – then gobbles it up.

Whipnose

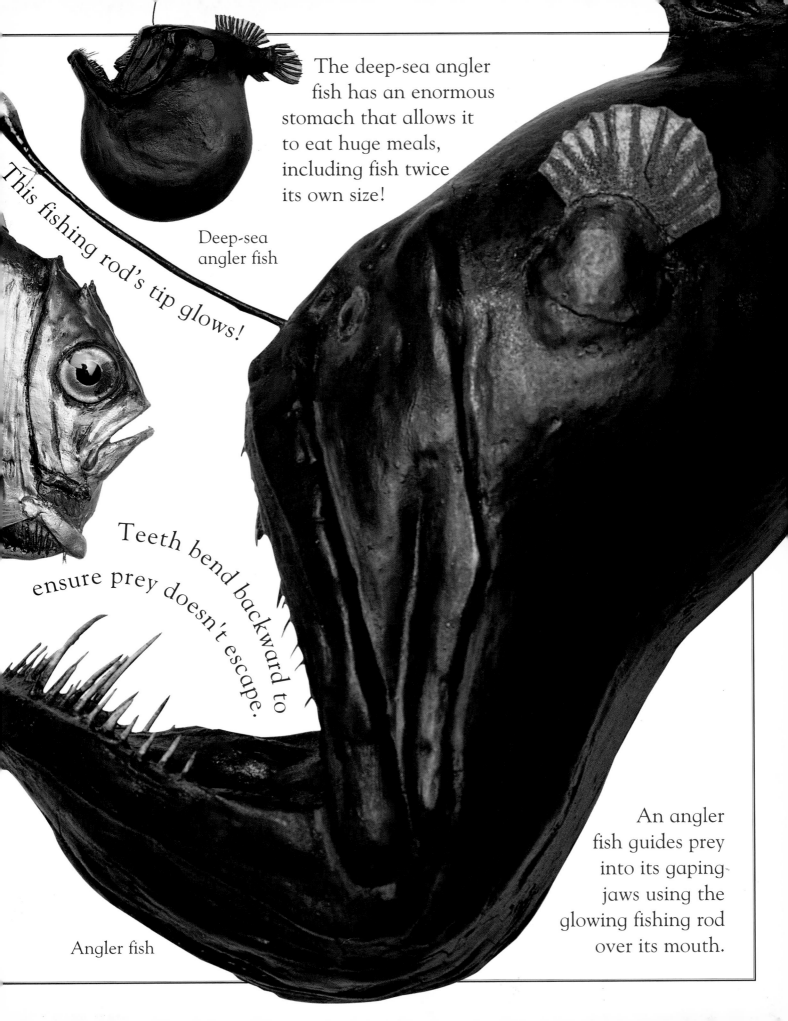

The deep-sea angler fish has an enormous stomach that allows it to eat huge meals, including fish twice its own size!

Deep-sea angler fish

This fishing rod's tip glows!

Teeth bend backward to ensure prey doesn't escape.

Angler fish

An angler fish guides prey into its gaping jaws using the glowing fishing rod over its mouth.

DEADLY POISONS

Bright colors and patterns are one way to send a warning to predators, saying: "I am deadly poisonous, so leave me alone!"

Mandarin fish

This fish raises the long spine on its back to look bigger and fiercer.

In Japan, people sometimes eat this deadly puffer fish – but only after a chef has taken out the poisonous parts!

Puffer fish

All sea snakes are poisonous. They inject poison into victims through fangs in the front of their mouths.

Sea snakes are more poisonous than land snakes.

Banded sea snake

The striking patterns of the mandarin fish remind predators of its slimy, smelly skin, which tastes horrible.

Extra-thick skin protects the fish from scratches.

This octopus paralyzes prey with its poisonous saliva.

Blue-ringed octopus

This tiny octopus is the same size as a person's hand, but it contains enough poison to kill 10 people!

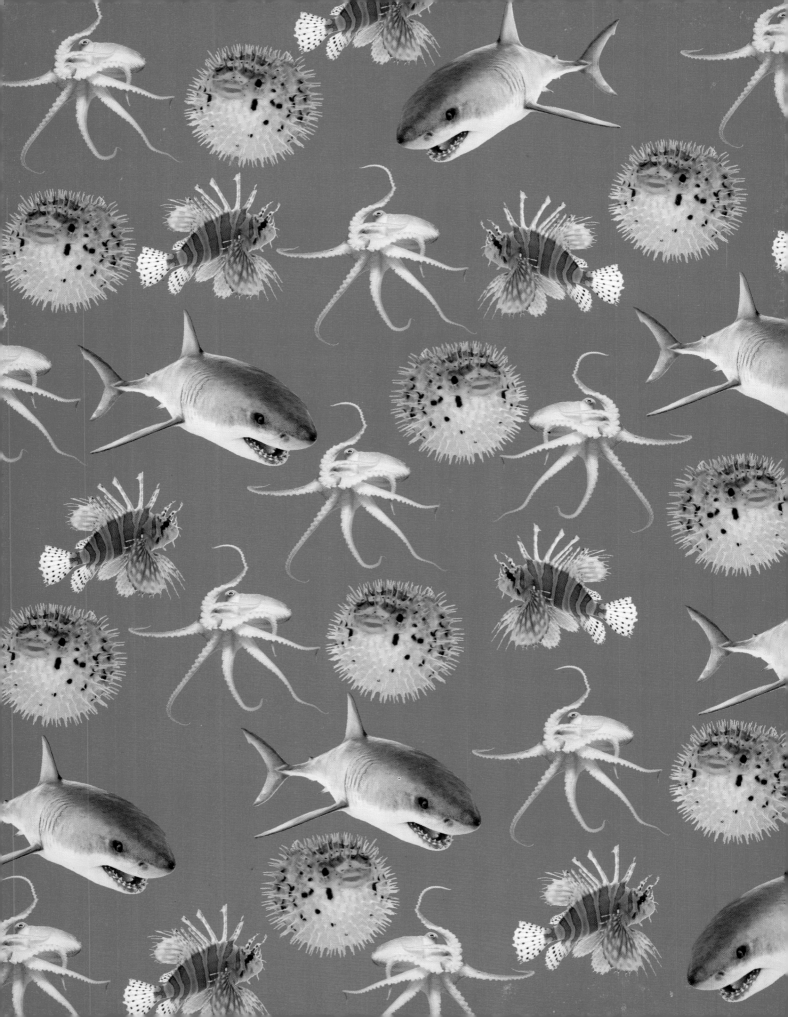